MINI MAKERS

by Lauren Kukla

raintree
a Capstone company — publishers for children

Raintree is an imprint of Capstone Global Library Limited, a company incorporated in England and Wales having its registered office at 264 Banbury Road, Oxford, OX2 7DY – Registered company number: 6695582

www.raintree.co.uk
myorders@raintree.co.uk

Hardback edition © Capstone Global Library Limited 2024
Paperback edition © Capstone Global Library Limited 2025
The moral rights of the proprietor have been asserted.

All rights reserved. No part of this publication may be reproduced in any form or by any means (including photocopying or storing it in any medium by electronic means and whether or not transiently or incidentally to some other use of this publication) without the written permission of the copyright owner, except in accordance with the provisions of the Copyright, Designs and Patents Act 1988 or under the terms of a licence issued by the Copyright Licensing Agency, 5th Floor, Shackleton House, 4 Battle Bridge Lane, London, SE1 2HX (www.cla.co.uk). Applications for the copyright owner's written permission should be addressed to the publisher.

Edited by: Jessica Rusick
Designed by: Aruna Rangarajan, Sarah DeYoung
Originated by Capstone Global Library Ltd

ISBN 978 1 3982 5169 4 (hardback)
ISBN 978 1 3982 5174 8 (paperback)

British Library Cataloguing in Publication Data
A full catalogue record for this book is available from the British Library.

Acknowledgements
We would like to thank the following for permission to reproduce photographs: iStockphoto: avean (font), Front Cover, 1, Back Cover; Mighty Media, Inc.: 5 (pencil), project photos; Shutterstock: donatas1205, 5 (right), Feng Yu, 5 (left), Photographee.eu, 7 (background), Prostock-studio, 9 (photograph), TabitaZn, Back Cover (gift tag)

Design Elements: iStockphoto: Tolga TEZCAN; Shutterstock: ds_vector, Valerii_M

Every effort has been made to contact copyright holders of material reproduced in this book. Any omissions will be rectified in subsequent printings if notice is given to the publisher.

All the internet addresses (URLs) given in this book were valid at the time of going to press. However, due to the dynamic nature of the internet, some addresses may have changed, or sites may have changed or ceased to exist since publication. While the author and publisher regret any inconvenience this may cause readers, no responsibility for any such changes can be accepted by either the author or the publisher.

CONTENTS

Mini machines 4

Mini spinny art... 6

Mini disco ball... 8

Mini wobbly UFO 10

Mini carousel spinner.................................... 12

Mini moving hedgehogs................................ 14

Mini rocket blast-off 16

Mini skateboards 18

Mini fan 20

Mini ferris wheel... 24

Mini prize wheel 28

Find out more 32

About the author.. 32

MINI MACHINES

Machines help us get around, do chores and have fun! But what if a machine were so little it could fit in the palm of your hand? Make some super-small machines to zoom and spin around your house or school.

You could make a **teeny-tiny skateboard** fit for a finger.

Craft a **super-small carousel** or a **mini Ferris wheel** for a cute carnival.

Or build a **cute hedgehog family** to scoot around your bedroom.

Whatever you create, these mini machine projects will help you **ZOOM** and **SPIN** your way to pocket-sized fun!

BASIC SUPPLIES

- » batteries
- » coloured card
- » craft foam
- » duct tape
- » glue stick
- » hot-glue gun
- » marker pens
- » mini hobby motors
- » paint and paintbrush
- » ruler
- » scissors

Crafting tips

SET YOURSELF UP FOR SUCCESS! Read through the materials and instructions before starting a project. Cover your workspace with paper or plastic to protect it from messes or spills.

LET YOUR CREATIVITY SHINE! Put your own stamp on these projects. Don't be afraid to make changes or try something new!

UPCYCLE! Lots of the projects in this book use materials you'll probably find around your home. Is there something you can't find? Think of ways to adapt the project using items you do have.

ASK FIRST! Get permission to do the projects and to use any materials you find at home or school.

SAFETY FIRST! Ask an adult for help with projects that require sharp or hot tools.

CLEAN UP! When you've finished crafting, make sure you put away any supplies you took out. Clean up any spills and wipe down your crafting surface.

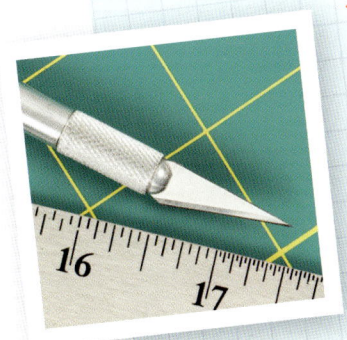

Mini SPINNY ART

Make a motorised spinning wheel to create some teeny weeny art!

MATERIALS

- » 1.5–6V mini hobby motor
- » battery pack with batteries
- » wire connectors
- » bottle lid
- » air-dry clay
- » jar lid
- » coloured card
- » scissors
- » cork
- » hot-glue gun
- » poster putty
- » marker pens

1

Insert the motor leads and battery pack leads into connectors. Attach the connectors. Both red wires and both black wires should align.

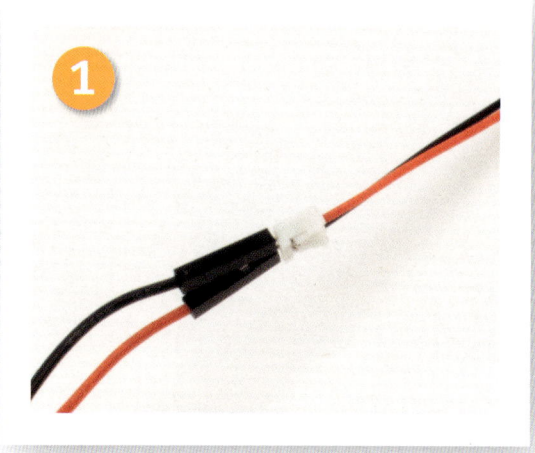

2

Pack the inside of the bottle lid with clay. Press the motor into the clay. Insert batteries into the battery pack.

3

Put the bottle lid in a small mound of clay. Press the clay around the lid. This will keep it steady when the motor is on.

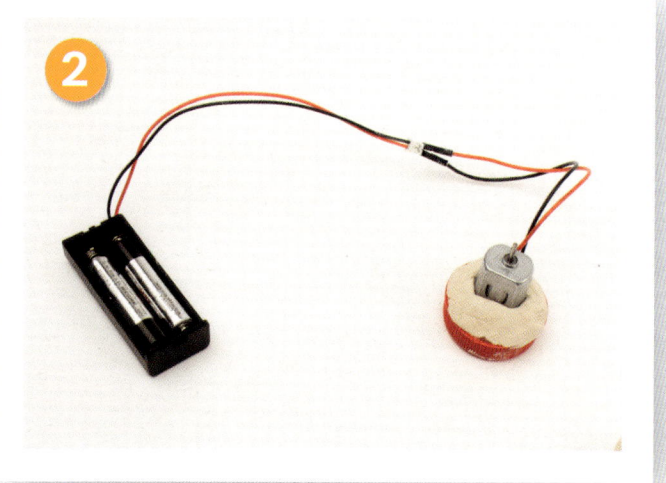

4

Trace the jar lid several times on coloured card and cut out the circles.

5

Cut a cork in half. Hot glue one half of the cork to the centre of the inside of the jar lid. Push the cork onto the motor's shaft.

6

Use poster putty to stick a paper circle onto the top of the jar lid. Turn on the motor so the paper circle spins. Gently press down on the paper with a marker pen to make a mini, spinny design!

Mini DISCO BALL

Get your celebration started with this tiny disco ball!

MATERIALS
- » 1.5–6V mini hobby motor
- » battery pack with batteries
- » wire connectors
- » jar lid
- » air-dry clay
- » push pin
- » rubber bouncy ball
- » hot-glue gun
- » sequins
- » paint and paintbrush

1

Insert the motor leads and battery pack leads into connectors. Attach the connectors. Both red wires and both black wires should align. Insert the batteries to make sure the motor works.

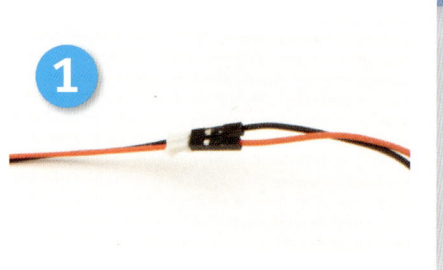

2

Pack the inside of the jar lid with clay. Press the motor into the clay.

3

Poke a push pin into the rubber bouncy ball.

4

Glue sequins around the bouncy ball. Start with larger sequins and fill in any gaps with smaller sequins.

5

Remove the push pin and push the bouncy ball onto the motor's shaft using the hole the push pin made.

6

Paint the clay after it dries. Then turn on the motor and watch the disco ball spin!

Mini WOBBLY UFO

Craft an out-of-this-world spacecraft for a teeny-tiny extraterrestrial!

MATERIALS

- » hammer and nail
- » jar lid
- » pencil with eraser
- » craft knife
- » 1.5–6V mini hobby motor
- » battery pack with batteries
- » wire connectors
- » hot-glue gun
- » electrical tape
- » coloured card
- » scissors
- » art supplies
- » double-sided foam tape

1

Ask an adult to help you use a hammer and nail to poke a hole in the centre of the jar lid.

2

Ask an adult to help you cut off the pencil's eraser using a craft knife.

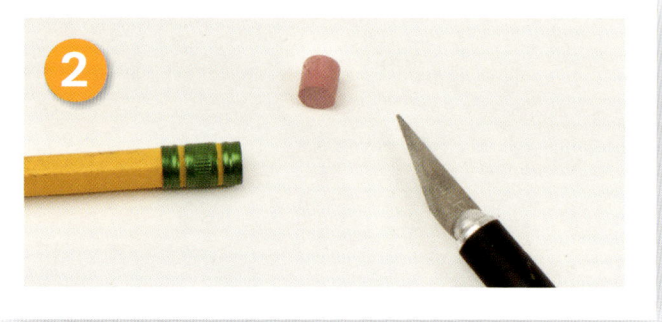

3

Insert the motor leads and battery pack leads into connectors. Attach the connectors. Both red wires and both black wires should align. Insert the batteries into the battery pack.

4

Poke the shaft of the motor through the hole in the jar lid and hot-glue the motor in place.

5

Attach the motor and battery pack to the top of the lid with electrical tape.

6

Push the pencil eraser onto the motor's shaft.

7

Cut a circle out of coloured card roughly the same size as the jar lid. Decorate it to look like a UFO. Add a paper alien if you like. Use double-sided foam tape to attach the circle to the top of the jar lid. Turn on the motor and watch your UFO wobble!

TINY TIP
Glue a paper wedge behind your alien if it won't stand on its own!

Mini CAROUSEL SPINNER

MATERIALS

- » washer
- » duct tape
- » craft knife
- » 4 toothpicks
- » scissors
- » ruler
- » paint and paintbrush (optional)
- » paper
- » hot-glue gun
- » art supplies
- » coloured card
- » marble

This miniature merry-go-round is the perfect addition to your next super-small carnival!

1

Cover a washer in duct tape. Use a craft knife to cut around the edges and middle. This will be the carousel's base.

2

Cut both pointed ends off the toothpicks. Trim each one so it is 4 centimetres long. Paint them if you like.

3

Cut a strip of paper 7.5 cm wide. Roll it to make a cone. Glue along the seam. Trim the bottom so the cone is 5 cm tall. This will be the carousel's roof. Decorate it if you like.

4

Glue the toothpicks so they are evenly spaced around the washer.

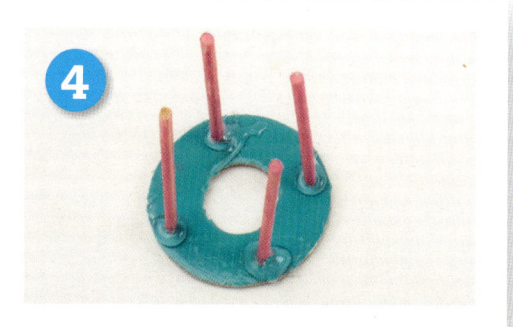

5

Cut out a coloured card circle the size of the washer. Glue it inside the cone. Then, glue the tops of the toothpicks to the cardboard circle.

6

Glue the marble to the bottom of the washer so it is centred inside the washer's hole. Spin your carousel and watch it go round and round!

TINY TIP
Decorate your carousel with scalloped paper or a small flag!

Mini MOVING HEDGEHOGS

Make a teeny tiny hedgehog that will wiggle and jiggle around your table!

MATERIALS

- » 3V single-cell battery
- » double-sided foam tape
- » scissors
- » mini vibrating motor
- » wire stripper
- » bottle lid
- » polymer clay
- » toothpicks
- » scissors
- » ruler
- » paint and paintbrush
- » oven
- » mini pom-poms
- » hot-glue gun

1
Cut a piece of double-sided foam tape the size of the battery.

2
Strip the ends of the motor's wires. Put the foam tape inside the bottle lid. Attach the red motor lead to the foam. Place the positive side of the battery on top of the wire.

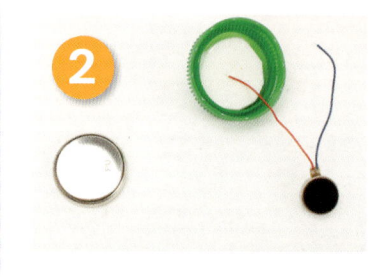

3
Shape a hedgehog out of clay.

4
Paint toothpicks and cut them into 0.5-to-1.5-cm pieces. Stick the dull ends into the hedgehog's back at an angle, making spines. Bake the hedgehog according to the clay's instructions.

5

Cut a piece of foam tape the size of the hedgehog and stick it to the hedgehog's underside.

6

Glue pom-poms around the outside edge of the bottle lid.

7

Stick the end of the black motor wire to the bottom of the hedgehog. Put your hedgehog on top of the battery and watch it wiggle!

TINY TIP
Make more hedgehogs for a little family!

Mini ROCKET BLAST-OFF

MATERIALS
- » plastic test tube
- » art supplies
- » scissors
- » paper
- » ruler
- » hot-glue gun
- » 3 toothpicks
- » cork
- » kitchen towel
- » bicarbonate of soda
- » measuring spoons
- » tape
- » vinegar

Shoot for the stars with this teeny-tiny test-tube bottle rocket!

1
Decorate a plastic test tube to look like a rocket.

2
Cut a strip of paper 8 cm wide. Roll it into a cone and glue along the seam. Trim the bottom so the cone is about 3 cm tall.

3
Glue the open end of the cone to the bottom of the test tube.

4
Cut three toothpicks 1.5 cm long. Space them evenly around the open end of the test tube and glue in place to make legs.

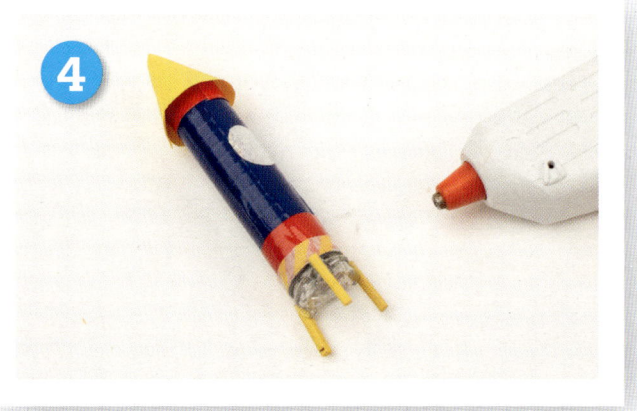

5

Cut a cork so it fits in the open end of the test tube.

6

Cut a strip of kitchen towel 8 cm long and 3 cm wide. Put ½ teaspoon bicarbonate of soda in the kitchen towel strip. Roll it up and tape the seam to make a small, skinny packet.

7

Fill the test tube halfway full with vinegar. Take the rocket outside. Insert the packet into the test tube and push in the cork. Stand the rocket on its legs and stand back to watch it blast off!

Mini SKATEBOARDS

Have fun doing finger flips and tricks with these super-small skateboards!

MATERIALS
- » wooden craft stick
- » scissors
- » ruler
- » cup of water
- » duct tape in 2 colours
- » drinking straw
- » toothpicks
- » pony beads
- » hot glue gun

1
Cut a wooden craft stick into 5-cm pieces.

2
Soak the pieces in water for 10 to 15 minutes.

3
Remove the stick pieces and use scissors to round their corners. Gently bend the pieces into curved skateboard shapes. Let them dry.

4
Stick a piece of duct tape on top of each skateboard. Trim off excess tape. Repeat with a different colour of tape on the bottoms of the skateboards.

TINY TIP
Use books or cardboard box flaps to make mini ramps for your skateboards!

5

Cut a drinking straw into 1.3-cm pieces. Glue two pieces to the bottom of each skateboard on opposite ends.

6

Cut toothpicks 2.5 cm long. Glue a bead to one end of each toothpick. Insert the open end of each toothpick through a straw segment and glue a second bead to the open end. Repeat with each straw segment. Your skateboards are ready to roll!

Mini FAN

Feeling hot? Craft a tiny fan to cool you off in a big way!

MATERIALS

- » cardboard tube
- » scissors
- » ruler
- » hole punch
- » 1.5–6V mini hobby motor with fan blade
- » hot-glue gun
- » duct tape
- » craft knife
- » battery pack with batteries
- » wire connectors
- » paper cup
- » wire
- » wire cutters
- » washer
- » button
- » art supplies

1

Cut lengths of cardboard tube 12.5 cm, 10 cm and 7.5 cm long.

2

Punch a hole near one edge of the 7.5-cm section. Repeat with the 12.5-cm section.

3

Thread the motor leads through the hole in the 7.5-cm section.

4

Glue the motor in place inside the tube. The motor's shaft should overhang the rim of the tube slightly.

5

Thread the leads through the 12.5-cm tube and out of the hole.

6

Set the 7.5-cm tube on top of the 12.5-cm tube to make a T shape. Secure with duct tape. This is the fan's head and neck.

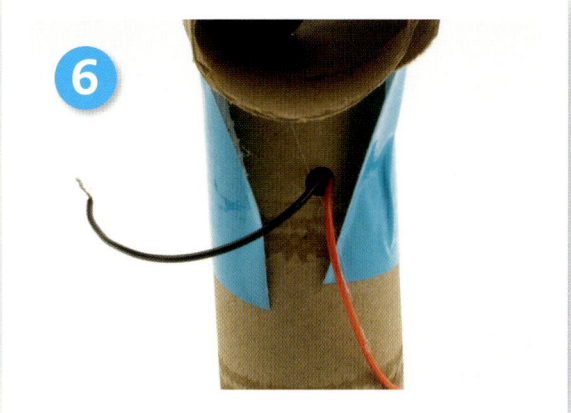

7

Cut the 10-cm tube in half lengthwise. Use a craft knife to cut a hole in the centre of one half so the neck can fit through. This will be the fan's base. Insert the fan's neck through the hole in the base and glue in place.

8

Insert the red motor lead and the red battery pack lead into a connector. Repeat with the black leads.

9

Cut 2.5 cm off the top of a paper cup, making a circle.

10

Using wire cutters, cut eight to ten lengths of wire 7.5 to 10 cm long.

11

Tape the end of one wire to the outside of the cup's rim. Stretch the wire across the rim and tape on the other side. Repeat with the other wires to make a fan cage.

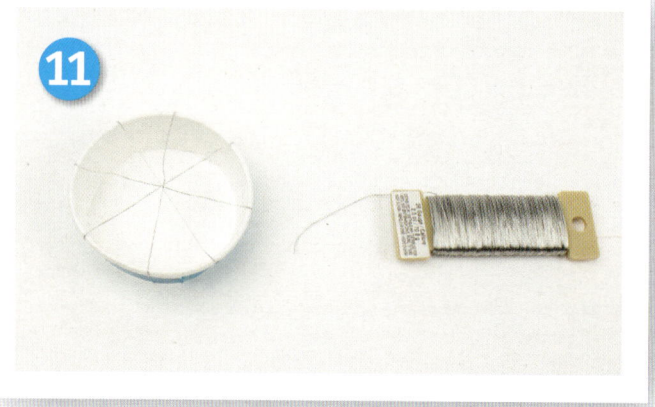

12

Glue a washer to the centre of the fan cage. Glue a button on top of the washer.

13

Push the fan blade onto the motor's shaft. Decorate the fan's head, neck and base if you like. Add batteries to the battery pack.

14

Glue the fan cage to the fan blade. Turn the fan on and cool off!

Mini FERRIS WHEEL

MATERIALS

- » plates in 2 different sizes
- » cardboard
- » pencil
- » ruler
- » craft knife
- » hot-glue gun
- » push pins
- » art supplies
- » cork
- » scissors
- » wooden skewer
- » drinking straw
- » paper cups
- » string

Send a small action figure or other toy round and round in this little Ferris wheel!

1

Trace the larger plate on a piece of cardboard to make a circle. Cut it out using a craft knife.

2

Use a ruler to draw a set of vertical lines down the centre of the circle. Draw a set of horizontal lines intersecting with the first set. Draw two more sets of lines so the circle is divided into eight equal sections.

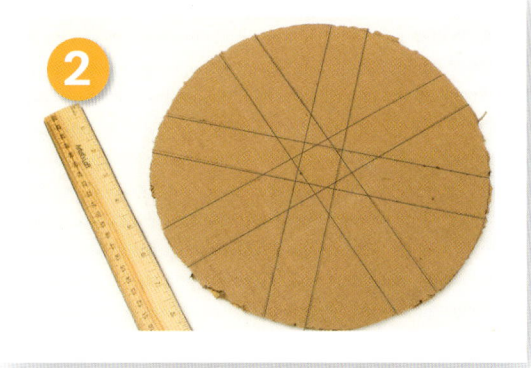

3

Centre a smaller plate in the circle and trace around it. You will now have eight pie-shaped sections inside a wheel shape.

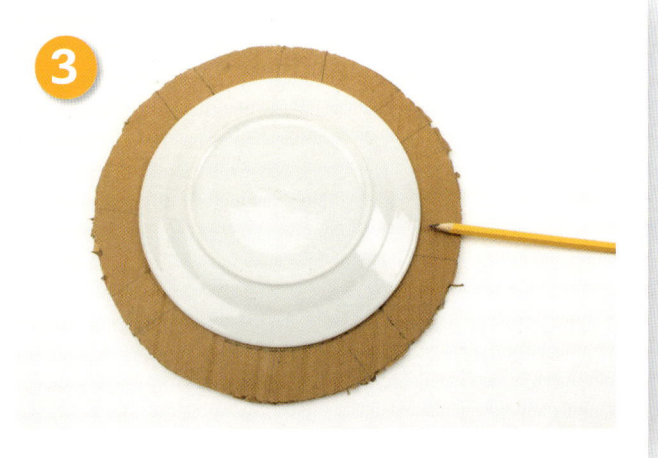

4

Cut the eight sections out of the wheel using a craft knife.

5

Cut a strip of cardboard 30 cm long and 7.5 cm wide. Cut another strip 18 cm long and 7.5 cm wide.

6

Fold the longer strip in half widthwise. Centre the ends on either long end of the smaller strip. Glue in place. This is the Ferris wheel's stand.

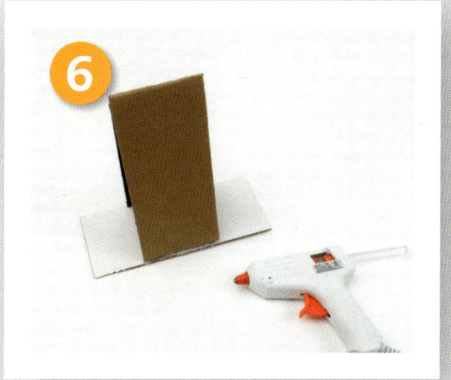

7

Use a push pin to poke a hole 2.5 cm from the top of the folded strip. Make sure the push pin goes through both halves of the strip. Use a pencil to widen the hole.

8

Use scrapbook paper, duct tape and other art supplies to decorate the wheel and base if you like.

9

Cut a cork in half. Push one half onto a wooden skewer.

10

Centre the cork on the back of the wheel and glue it in place.

11

Cut a section of drinking straw 5 cm long. Push the section through both holes in the stand and glue in place.

12

Insert the free end of the skewer through the straw.

13

Cut the top off a paper cup so it is 2.5 cm tall. Cut a small door in the front. This will be a Ferris wheel car.

14

Repeat step 13 to make seven more Ferris wheel cars.

15

Cut eight lengths of string that are 5 cm long. Glue each piece of string to the back of a car, making a loop.

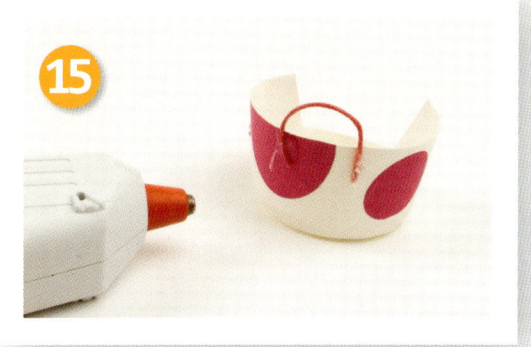

16

Space eight push pins evenly around the wheel. Hang the loop of each car off a push pin. Spin your wheel and watch it go!

Mini PRIZE WHEEL

Spin it to win it with this super-small prize wheel!

MATERIALS

- » jar lid
- » cardboard
- » pencil
- » scissors
- » ruler
- » hot glue gun
- » coloured paper
- » glue stick
- » marker pen
- » white paper
- » push pin
- » screw
- » 8 toothpicks
- » nut and washer
- » craft foam
- » miscellaneous prizes

1

Trace a jar lid on a piece of cardboard. Cut out the circle.

2

Cut a strip of cardboard 7.5 cm wide and 30 cm long. Fold into thirds to make a triangle. Hot glue the edges together. This is the prize wheel's stand.

3

Trace the jar lid on eight different colours of paper. Cut out the circles.

4

Attach a paper circle to the cardboard circle using a glue stick.

5

Fold a second paper circle in half and cut along the crease. Glue one half on top of the cardboard circle so it overlaps the first paper circle.

6

Fold two more circles into quarters and cut along the creases. Glue two quarter pieces on top of the wheel so it is divided into four different colours.

7

Fold the final four circles into eighths. Cut one eighth piece out of each circle. Arrange the pieces on top of the cardboard circle to make a wheel with eight equal sections in different colours and patterns.

8

Write numbers 1 to 8 on white paper. Cut out the numbers and glue one number to each segment of the wheel.

9

Use a push pin to poke a hole in the wheel's centre. Use a pencil to widen it until a screw can fit through. The wheel should turn freely around the screw.

10

Cut a 1.3-cm piece off the end of each toothpick. Use a push pin to poke a hole near the top of each wheel section. Push the point of each toothpick piece into the holes.

11

Use a push pin to poke a hole through the centre of the cardboard stand, near the top edge. Use a pencil to widen it until a screw can fit through.

12

Put a washer on the screw and push the screw through the hole in the centre of the wheel, then through the hole in the cardboard stand. Use a nut to secure the screw in place.

13

Cut a small triangle shape out of craft foam. Round one end. Hot glue the rounded end to the top of a push pin.

14

Stick the push pin into the bottom of the stand so the pointed end of the foam can touch the toothpicks.

15

Assign a different prize or reward for each number. Invite your friends to spin the wheel to see what they win!

FIND OUT MORE

BOOKS

Simple Machines at the Theme Park (Theme Park Science), Tammy Enz (Raintree, 2020)

Spring Crafts From Different Cultures (Multicultural Seasonal Crafts), Megan Borgert-Spaniol (Raintree, 2023)

Upcycled Plastic Projects (Eco Crafts), Marcy Morin and Heidi E Thompson (Raintree, 2022)

WEBSITES

www.bbc.co.uk/cbeebies/makes/lets-go-club-ten-minute-crafts?collection=the-lets-go-club-craft-activities
The CBeebies website has lots of quick craft activities to do.

www.goodhousekeeping.com/home/craft-ideas/g39762537/crafts-for-kids/
Find ideas for some easy craft activities on this website.

www.sciencefun.org/kidszone/experiments/force-and-motion-science-experiments/
This website has lots of science-based craft ideas to make.

ABOUT THE AUTHOR

Lauren Kukla is a poet and an author of books and media for children. She loves embroidery, walking, camping and growing vegetables in her garden. She lives in Minneapolis, Minnesota, USA, with her husband, two small kids, a silly white dog and four city chickens. You can follow her poetry on Instagram @NorthCountryPoet.